FOCUS ON
Comprehension 4

Nelson

FICTION						NON-FICTION						
Classic fiction	Adaptation for TV or film	Range of genres	Classic poetry	Range of poetry	Classic drama	Autobiography/biography	Journalistic writing	Reports	Discussion texts	Formal writing	Explanations	Reference text
						✓	✓	✓				
		✓	✓					✓				
✓	✓	✓										
			✓									
						✓	✓	✓		✓		
✓		✓										
			✓	✓								
✓		✓										
			✓									
						✓	✓				✓	
									✓			
				✓								
			✓									
			✓									
✓	✓	✓										
							✓	✓	✓			
			✓									
✓		✓										
										✓	✓	
✓		✓										
✓	✓	✓				✓	✓					
✓		✓										

Contents

Unit 1	Long Wolf	*page* 4
Unit 2	How Can You Buy the Sky?	6
Unit 3	The Demon Headmaster	8
Unit 4	Such a Stubborn Mule!	10
Unit 5	A Day in the Life of a Bethlehem Shepherd	12
Unit 6	It's too Frightening for Me	15
Unit 7	The Hippocrump	18
Unit 8	The Iron Woman	21
Unit 9	The Kangaroo's Coff	24
Unit 10	The First Man to Swim the Channel	26
Unit 11	The Business Letter	29
Unit 12	Twelfth Night	31
Unit 13	Amanda	34
Unit 14	In the Stable: A Christmas Haiku	36
Unit 15	Christmas Dinner	38
Unit 16	The Fuss over the Fordham Factory	41
Unit 17	There's a Dragon	44
Unit 18	Trash or Treasure?	46
Unit 19	Sleep	50
Unit 20	Cluny's Army	54
Unit 21	Robinson Crusoe's Diary	58
Unit 22	The Mysterious Postcard	62

UNIT 1   Long Wolf

Think ahead

Do you think this passage is going to be about an animal or a person? Why?

Long Wolf Goes Home

Chief Long Wolf fought with the Sioux against the US army and, according to his family, helped to defeat General Custer at Little Big Horn in 1876. When the Sioux were finally overcome, however, he joined 'Buffalo Bill' Cody's Wild West Show.

In 1892 he contracted pneumonia on a trip to London to perform at Earls Court, died, and was buried by Cody at Brompton Cemetery, where his grave has lain untended for decades. His body, which was examined at the West London Hospital, was covered with wounds and sabre scars believed to have been inflicted during battles with the US Cavalry.

Yesterday, Jessie Black Feather, 87, the grand-daughter and oldest descendant of Long Wolf, said: 'We have come to England to fulfil my grandfather's dying wish to be returned to America.' Jessie's mother, Lizzie, was 12 and with her father in London when he died. The family was unable to take his body home immediately, and after she returned to America she lost track of where Long Wolf was buried.

His body will be exhumed on Thursday, taken in a horse-drawn carriage to the gates of the cemetery, then flown home. He will be buried on Sunday with Indian and Christian ceremonies at the ancestral burial ground of the Ogala Sioux tribe at Pine Ridge Reservation in Wounded Knee.

The trail to Long Wolf's repatriation began six years ago when Elizabeth Knight from Bromsgrove found a book in an antique shop by Robert Cunningham Graham, the adventurer and politician. It contained a long passage on the life and lonely death of Long Wolf, and described how the once-great Sioux chief lay in a 'neglected grave in a lone corner of a crowded London cemetery.'

Mrs Knight set to work, found Long Wolf's grave, and tracked down his descendants by placing adverts in American newspapers. John Black Feather, the son of Jessie and great grandson of the chief said: 'I couldn't believe it when I spotted this advert; my mother had been searching for years for her grandfather's grave. We were so excited.'

The bureaucratic process, which lasted four years, began with letters to the US State Department and the British Government.

'As he lay dying, the chief said how much he wanted to go home,' said John Black Feather. 'We're just delighted now that we have almost fulfilled his wish. We do not believe his spirit will be settled until his body has been brought home.'

Adapted from an article in *The Times* (September 23, 1997) by Philip Delves Broughton

Thinking back

1 Who was Long Wolf?
2 Why did he come to Britain?
3 How and when did he die?
4 Where was he buried?
5 What was Long Wolf's dying wish?
6 Who came to England to take Long Wolf home?
7 Where will Long Wolf be buried in America?
8 Who found Long Wolf's grave and contacted his descendants?

 Thinking about it

1 Who were the Sioux?
2 How do you know the Sioux did not win their fight against General Custer?
3 What do you think 'Buffalo Bill' Cody's Wild West Show was?
4 Why do you think Long Wolf's grave had lain untended for decades?
5 What do you think made Elizabeth Knight do everything she did?
6 What was John Black Feather's reaction when he saw the advert about Long Wolf in the newspaper?
7 What do you think John Black Feather meant when he said, 'We do not believe his spirit will be settled until his body has been brought home'?

 Thinking it through

1 Do you believe this story is true or false? Say why.
2 Were you glad the story had a happy ending? Say why.
3 Use a dictionary if necessary. Write what these words mean:
   a) neglected   b) descendants   c) exhumed   d) repatriation
4 Why do you think Long Wolf and Jessie Black Feather were given their names?
5 Why do you think the Sioux Indians would have been fighting the US Army?

UNIT 2   How can you buy the Sky?

Is it really possible to buy the sky? What do you think?

Chief Seattle spoke these words in 1855 to the US government when they wanted to buy the lands of his native American people.

How can you buy the sky?

The voice of my ancestors said to me,
The shining water that moves in the streams and the rivers
is not simply water, but the blood of your grandfather's
  grandfather.
Each ghostly reflection in the clear waters on the lake
tells of memories in the life of our people.
The water's murmur is the voice of your great-great-grandmother,
The rivers are your brothers. They quench our thirst.
They carry our canoes and feed our children.
You must give the rivers kindness
you would give any brother.

The voice of my grandfather said to me,
The air is precious. It shares its spirit with all the life it supports.
The wind that gave me my first breath also received my last sigh.
You must keep the land and the air apart and sacred,
as a place where one can go to taste the wind
that is sweetened by the meadow flowers.

When the last Red Man and Woman have
  vanished with their wilderness,
and their memory is only the shadow of
  a cloud moving across the prairie,
will the shores and forests still be there?
Will there be any of the spirit
  of my people left?
My ancestors said to me, This we know:
The earth does not belong to us.
  We belong to the earth.

Thinking back

1 When did Chief Seattle speak the words of the poem?
2 Who was he speaking to?
3 Why was he speaking to them?
4 Why did the voice of his ancestors say that rivers were important?
5 What did his grandfather say was precious?

 Thinking about it

1 What do you think Chief Seattle means when he asks how you can buy the sky?
2 Why do you think he remembers all the things his ancestors have told him?
3 Chief Seattle says the water is the 'blood of your grandfather's grandfather'. What could this mean?
4 How can water be seen as the life-blood of our planet?
5 What does the last line of the poem mean?

 Thinking it through

1 As far as we know Chief Seattle could not read or write. His spoken words were translated and written down for him. Do you think his words are a poem? Give your reasons.
2 Do you agree that this poem is about conservation? Explain your answer.
3 In your own words, say how Chief Seattle feels about the environment and what his concerns might be about the future.
4 Chief Seattle seems to think the earth has a living spirit. Do you agree? Say why.

UNIT 3   The Demon Headmaster

Think ahead

From this title, what sort of picture do you get of the Headmaster?

'The Headmaster will see you,' he said. 'Follow me.'

Thoroughly bewildered now, Dinah walked into the school after him and along a straight corridor. At her old school, all the walls had been covered with pictures and drawings done by the pupils, but these walls were completely blank, except for a framed notice hung halfway along. Dinah swivelled her head to read it as she passed.

> **The man who can keep order can rule the world.**

Frowning slightly, she went on following Jeff until he came to a stop in front of a door which had the single word HEADMASTER painted on it. He knocked.

'Come in.'

Jeff pushed the door open and waved Dinah inside, pulling it shut behind her.

As she stepped through, Dinah glanced quickly round the room. It was the tidiest office she had ever seen. There were no papers, no files, no pictures on the walls. Just a large empty-topped desk, a filing cabinet and a bookcase with a neat row of books.

She took it all in in one second and then forgot it as her eyes fell on the man standing by the window. He was tall and thin, dressed in an immaculate black suit. From his shoulders, a long, black teacher's gown hung in heavy folds, like wings, giving him the appearance of a huge crow. Only his head was startlingly white. His eyes were hidden behind dark glasses, like two black holes in the middle of the whiteness.

She cleared her throat. 'Hello. I'm Dinah Glass and I – '

He raised a long, ivory-coloured hand. 'Please do not speak until you are asked. Idle chatter is an inefficient waste of energy.'

Unnervingly he went on staring at her for a moment or two without saying anything else. Dinah wished she could see the eyes behind the dark lenses...

From *The Demon Headmaster* by Gillian Cross

Thinking back

1 What was the girl's name?
2 Who took her to see the Headmaster?
3 In what way was the corridor different from her old school?
4 What notice was on the corridor wall?
5 What were Dinah's first impressions of the Headmaster's office?
6 Describe how the Headmaster looked.

Thinking about it

1 Why do you think Dinah is at the school?
2 Why do you think Dinah 'frowned slightly' when she read the notice?
3 What does the way the Headmaster's office is organised tell you about him?
4 What gave the Headmaster 'the appearance of a crow'?
5 What can you tell about the Headmaster from:
   a) the way he dresses   b) the things he says and does?

Thinking it through

1 Write what some of Dinah's thoughts and feelings would have been as:
   a) she walked down the corridor   b) she first stepped into the office   c) she first saw the Headmaster.
2 Did the author make you feel uncomfortable when you read the passage? How? Why?
3 Imagine you are a new child coming into your school for the first time. Describe what your impressions might be as:
   a) you walk in   b) go into your Head Teacher's office
   c) you meet your Head Teacher for the first time.

UNIT 4   Such a Stubborn Mule!

Think ahead

Where do you think the story is set? Why?

One day the Hodja (a scholar of religious law) told his wife to go and feed his donkey. She refused, saying that that was his work. They agreed that whichever of them spoke first should go and do it.

The Hodja sat in a corner and said nothing. His wife went to visit a neighbour and told her what had happened.

'He is such a stubborn mule!' she said. 'He'll die of hunger rather than speak.'

'I will send him some soup,' said her friend, and sent her son with some for him.

In the meantime, however, a thief broke into their house and began to put things of value into his bag. When the Hodja saw the thief he made no sound or movement, so the thief thought he must be paralysed. The thief carried on stealing everything of value and even stole the Hodja's *kavuk* (hat) from his head! Then he left.

Soon afterwards, the boy arrived with the soup. The Hodja was determined not to speak so he pointed to his head and mimed how the thief had stolen his hat. The boy did not understand and thought the Hodja was asking him to pour his soup on his head – which he did! The Hodja was furious but he still said nothing!

The boy went back home, and reported everything he had seen. The Hodja's wife realised something was wrong, and hurried home as fast as she could. When she entered the house and saw the mess, she cried, 'What has happened?'

'I've won! I've won!' rejoiced the Hodja. 'You feed the donkey!' Then he remembered the thief. 'But look what trouble your obstinacy has caused!' he said.

Thinking back

Finish each sentence with a sensible ending.
1 The Hodja was tired of feeding _____ .
2 The Hodja's wife said that feeding the donkey was _____ .
3 The wife's friend sent the Hodja _____ .
4 A thief stole the Hodja's _____ .
5 The boy misunderstood the Hodja and poured the soup

_____ .
6 When the boy told the Hodja's wife, she _____ .
7 The Hodja said _____ .
8 The Hodja told his wife that she was _____ .

 Thinking about it

1 Write three things you have learnt about the character of the
  Hodja. Give your reasons.
2 Write some things you have discovered about:
  a) the Hodja's wife   b) his wife's friend   c) the thief
3 Why do you think the boy misunderstood the Hodja?
  How could he have made himself clearer do you think?
4 What do you think made his wife realise the Hodja's house
  had been burgled?
5 Why did the Hodja rejoice when his wife spoke?

 Thinking it through

1 What moral do you think we can learn from this story?
2 What do you think the reaction of the Hodja's wife was at the
  end of the story?
3 What is your opinion of the Hodja? Explain your answer.
4 In what ways are we able to communicate with others without
  actually speaking?
5 Did you enjoy the story? What did you think of it?

UNIT 5   A Day in the Life of a Bethlehem Shepherd

Think ahead

What does a shepherd do?
What do you think a shepherd's job would be like?

My job is the best job in the world. I started to learn it from the age of seven from my father, who learnt it from his father. In my youth one could stroll freely, without limits. You did not have to stop and think, 'Is this my land, or does it belong to someone else?' Now my herding zone is restricted to a day's  circle within the area of Bethlehem. This is sad for me. I wish it was like the old times when I was free to go anywhere.

I have 100 sheep and a few goats. All of them have names and understand me when I call them. I do care about them, but I also know that I have to sacrifice them in order to survive.

My bed is in the open field on the hills of Beit Sahur. It is a raised steel platform, where I lie, covered in woollen blankets, next to my flock in their wooden enclosure. There is a small stone shelter nearby in case of rain.

As soon as I wake up, before sunrise, I open the gate for the goats and sheep and tell them to go out on the hillside. I walk with them, searching for areas where they can graze. In the spring, when the land is greener, the food is quite plentiful, but during the long, dry summers the vegetation is often sparse and I have to give the sheep extra grain. For most of the year the hills are brown and barren.

But to me and my forefathers they have supported us and been our home for centuries.

I continue these walks until about 11 a.m., when the animals are ready for a rest. Then I return to the area I have fenced off for their protection, and I give them water.

My first meal is usually tea with bread and laban (goat's milk yogurt). This is my favourite meal of the day. Then I feed the flock with grains and I sit, watching over them, for about four hours. I stand up only when I hear a noise and need to check if they are being threatened by a fox or some other animal. I have placed scarecrows around my enclosure to frighten away predators, but I also have to watch out for robbers. You can't trust anyone these days.

At about 3 p.m. I lead them out into the fields again and we restart the search for food. As we walk along I sing and recite poetry, although I have never learnt to read and write. I think poetry is very soothing and relaxing. I walk with the sheep until seven, when night has fallen. Then I herd them back into the fold to rest and I wait for my children to bring my dinner, which is usually meat – beef or lamb – and some vegetables.

After dinner I sit and gaze up at the stars. To me, this is one of the best parts of the day, when I can simply sit and think. By looking at the sky, I can tell whether the next day will bring rain or be hot. I say my final prayer at 8 p.m., having already prayed four times during the day – in the morning, at midday, and at three and five. I stay in the fields, watching over my flock, counting the sheep, to make sure they are all safe and secure. My family sleeps in a stone house nearby.

When I have other chores to do I leave my sons to watch over the flock. I think my job is hard and I need their help, especially during the milking season, between March and May, when I work with my wives and some of my children making cheese. We have to clean and purify the milk before stirring it. When it has been transformed into cheese we cover it with white paper and press until all the water is removed. We add salt and place the cheese into bags. The next morning, I get up at three to pack the bags on a donkey and take them to market in Bethlehem. There is nothing quite like the taste of my cheese. It's wonderful.

Adapted from an article in *The Sunday Times Magazine* (December 21, 1997) by Ross Dunn

Thinking back

Copy these sentences and complete the gaps with suitable words.

Ahmed Abyyiat is a shepherd in __1__ . He loves his job.
Ahmed's __2__ taught him how to be a shepherd from the age of
__3__ . Ahmed has 100 sheep and some __4__ . Each sheep has its
own __5__ . Ahmed sleeps on a raised __6__ platform. He has a
small stone shelter in case it __7__ . Before sunrise Ahmed takes
the sheep to __8__ on the hillside. Around 11 o'clock he returns
to the __9__ and gives them some __10__ .

 Thinking about it

1 Make up a timetable for a normal day for Ahmed. For example,
  at 6 a.m. he gets up and prays.
2 List some things that make Ahmed happy.
3 Why does Ahmed have to give the sheep extra grain in the
  summer?
4 What are the main dangers to the sheep?
5 What part of the day do you think Ahmed likes best?
6 Describe briefly how Ahmed makes cheese.

 Thinking it through

1 Do you think Ahmed finds his job a lonely one? Why?
2 A fact is something that is true and can be proved. An
  opinion is what a person thinks – it may or may not be true
  (such as, Ahmed says that his job is the best job in the world).
  Find four opinions expressed by Ahmed.
3 Write some of the things you found surprising about Ahmed.
4 Use a dictionary if necessary. Write what the following words
  mean: a) turbulent b) enclosure c) graze
  d) vegetation e) sparse f) barren g) predators
5 List what you think are some of the good and bad things
  about being a shepherd.

UNIT 6   It's too Frightening for Me

Think ahead

What sort of a story might this be?

There were spooks in there. Jim and Arthur knew this for sure because they had heard the ghostly screams.

Sometimes they dared one another to squeeze through the gate, where the bars had rusted away, and creep up the overgrown drive. Thick bushes grew on either side, dripping and rustling.

Round the corner, the drive opened out into a bit of garden where a crumbling porch tottered over the front door. There were little windows on either side of it with cracked panes of coloured glass. But Jim and Arthur never got a closer look before the screaming started. It came from the letter box, high and shrill.

'Go away, go away, go awayeeeeeee ...' it screamed.

Jim and Arthur never waited to find out what was going to happen next.

'It's a spook!' little Arthur would say, his eyes wide with fright. 'There's a horrible witch in there. Don't let's ever go there again, Jim.'

But somehow neither of them could keep away for long.

Arthur had some nasty thoughts about the house in his bed at night. Jim always pretended not to mind about that sort of thing ...

The two brothers go back to the house on another day. They see a girl looking out of the window. Jim decides to find out more. Little Arthur decides to follow.

Up a shadowy flight of stairs and into a large hall crept Arthur, expecting to be pounced on at any moment.

There were a great many doors leading off the hall. Arthur paused. He heard voices. He peered through the crack in one of the doors. Then he opened it a tiny bit, and a little wider, and peered around ... and there, as large as life, was that cheeky Jim! He was sitting on the floor, in a room full of furniture muffled in dust sheets, talking to a fair-haired girl. He had forgotten all about Arthur!

Arthur felt like punching Jim, but he couldn't because Jim was bigger than he was. Besides, he wanted to find out more about this girl. She looked rather nice, though a little skinny. She was certainly not a spook.

Jim started to explain. 'This is Mary and she ...'

But at this moment the terrible ghostly screaming was heard in the hall. It was just outside the door!

In rushed a bony figure, all in black and wild white hair, waving its stick-like arms about and gobbling like a goose in between screams.

'Go away – AAAAH – go away – SHRIEK – I'll have no lads in here – AAAAUGH, gobble, gobble, gob – get out, GET OUT!'

Jim and Arthur both dived under a dust-sheet and crouched there, like a couple of ghosts themselves. They were trapped.

But Mary was speaking calmly. 'Come on, Gran, behave yourself. What about a nice cup of tea, then?'

It wasn't a witch. It was Mary's Granny, but she was very nearly as frightening. Peeping out from their sheet, Jim and Arthur saw Mary take her hand.

Slowly the screaming stopped. Mary managed to coax the old lady down to the kitchen and sat her in her chair. Not knowing quite what to do, Jim and Arthur followed.

While Granny sipped her tea, still gobbling and mumbling into her cup, Mary explained that she was having one of her 'turns'.

From *Too Frightening For Me* by Shirley Hughes

Thinking back

Match up the sentence beginnings and endings. Write each sentence correctly in your book.

1 Jim and Arthur heard screams   and left Arthur outside.
2 They always ran away   and stopped her screaming.
3 Arthur thought there was   was having a 'turn'.
4 One day the two boys saw   when they heard the screams.
5 Jim went in to find the girl   coming from the house.
6 The boys dived under   a girl at one of the windows.
7 Mary sat her Gran in a chair   a dust sheet.
8 Mary explained that her Gran   a witch in the house.

Thinking about it

1 The passage has been broken into two parts, like chapters. Explain what each part is mainly about.
2 Which of the two boys do you think was older? Why?
3 The boys were frightened of the house but 'somehow neither of them could keep away for long.' Why?
4 Which of the two boys do you think was braver? Why?
5 Describe: a) Mary   b) her Gran
6 Why were Arthur and Jim 'like a couple of ghosts' when they were under the dust sheet?
7 What caused Mary's Granny to have one of her 'turns'?

Thinking it through

1 Did you like the author's style of writing? Explain your answer.
2 List some of the words the author uses to give the passage a creepy feeling.
3 What do you think life would be like for Mary?
4 How would Mary have felt when she saw Arthur and Jim? Why?
5 Write a description of how you imagine:
   a) the house looked from the outside
   b) what it was like inside.

UNIT 7   The Hippocrump

Think ahead

The Hippocrump is a kind of animal. Do you think it is real or imaginary? Is it going to be friendly or fierce?

Along the valley of the Ump
Gallops the fearful Hippocrump.
His hide is leathery and thick;
His eyelids open with a Click!
His mouth he closes with a Clack!
He has three humps upon his back;
On each of these there grows a score
Of horny spikes, and sometimes more.
His hair is curly, thick and brown;
Beneath his chin a beard hangs down.
He has eight feet with hideous claws;
His neck is long – and O his jaws!
The boldest falters in his track
To hear those hundred teeth go Clack!

The Hippocrump is fierce indeed,
But if it eats the baneful weed
That grows beside the Purple Lake,
His hundred teeth begin to ache.
Then how the creature stamps and roars
Along the Ump's resounding shores!
The drowsy cattle faint with fright;
The birds fall flat, the fish turn white.
Even the rocks begin to shake;
The children in their beds awake;
The old ones quiver, quail and quake.
'Alas!' they cry. 'Make no mistake,
It is Himself – he's got the Ache
From eating by the Purple Lake!'
Some say, 'It is old You-know-who -
He's in a rage: what shall we do?'
'Lock up the barns, protect the stores,
Bring all the pigs and sheep indoors!'

18

They call upon their god, Agw-ump
To save them from the Hippocrump.
'What's that I hear go hop-skip-jump?
He's coming! Stand aside there!' Bump!
Lump-lump! – He's on the bridge now – Lump!
'I hear his tail' – ker-flump, ker-flump!
'I see the prickles on his hump!
It is, it is – the Hippocrump!
Defend us now, O Great Agw-ump!'

Thus prayed the dwellers by the Ump.
Their prayer was heard. A broken stump
Caught the intruder in the rump.
He slipped into the foaming river,
Whose icy water quenched his fever,
Then while the creature floundering lay,
The timid people ran away;
And when the morrow dawned serene
The Hippocrump was no more seen.
Glad hymns of joy the people raised:
'For ever Great Agw-ump be praised!'

From *The Hippocrump* by James Reeves

 Thinking back

**Say if these statements are true (T), false (F) or if you
can't tell (CT).**
1 The Hippocrump has two humps on its back.
2 The Hippocrump has a beard.
3 The Hippocrump sleeps in a cave.
4 The weed by the lake gives the Hippocrump toothache.
5 When the creature is in a rage it stamps and roars.
6 The noise of the angry Hippocrump wakes up the children.
7 The people pray to their god to keep them safe.
8 The Hippocrump slipped on a muddy patch.

Thinking about it

1 In your own words, write a description of the Hippocrump.
2 What effect does the weed at the Purple Lake have on the Hippocrump?
3 How can people tell the Hippocrump is in a rage without even seeing it?
4 What effect does the angry Hippocrump have on:
   a) animals   b) rocks   c) sleeping children   d) old people?
5 Do you think the people have seen the Hippocrump in a rage before? Why?
6 a) Why did the people pray to their god?
   b) How did they think their prayers were answered?
   c) How did they thank Agw-ump?
7 How do you think the people felt:
   a) when they ran away   b) when they returned next day?

 Thinking it through

1 Say something you liked or disliked about the poem.
2 Give the poem marks out of ten. Explain why you gave your marks.
3 The poem is divided into four verses. Briefly say what the main theme of each verse is.
4 What do you think of the poet's description of the Hippocrump in verse 1? Why?
5 If you had been there, how could you have saved the people from the Hippocrump?
6 Use a dictionary if necessary. Write the meaning of these words:
   a) hideous   b) falters   c) baneful   d) resounding
   e) quail   f) intruder   g) flounder   h) serene

UNIT 8　The Iron Woman

Think ahead
Who, or what, will The Iron Woman be like?

Then it came again. Beneath her feet the bridge road jumped and the rail jarred her hand. At the same moment, the water surface of the drain was blurred by a sudden mesh of tiny ripples all over it.

An earthquake! It must be an earthquake!

A completely new kind of fear gripped Lucy. For a few seconds she did not dare to move. The thought of the bridge collapsing and dropping her into the drain with its writhing eels was bad enough. But the thought of the marsh itself opening a great crack, and herself and all the water and mud and eels and reeds pouring into bottomless black, maybe right into the middle of the earth, was worse. She felt her toes curling like claws and the soles of her feet prickling with electricity.

Quickly then she began to walk – but it was like walking on a bouncy narrow plank between skyscrapers. She lifted each foot carefully and set it down firmly yet gently. As fast as she dared, and yet quite slow. But soon – she couldn't help it – she started running. What if the earthquake shock had brought the ceiling down on her mother? Or even shaken the village flat, like dominoes. And what if some great towering piece of machinery, at the factory, had toppled on her father?

And then, as she ran, it came again, pitching her off balance, so that her left foot hit her right calf and down she went. As she lay there, flat and winded, it came again. This time, the road seemed to hit her chest and stomach, a strong, hard thump. Then another. And each time, she saw the road gravel under her face jump slightly. And it was then, as she lay there, that she heard the weirdest sound. Nothing like any bird she had ever heard. It came from out of the marsh behind her. It was a long, wailing cry, like a fire-engine siren. She jumped up and began to run blindly

Already the head was out. It didn't look much like a head – simply a gigantic black lump, crowned with reeds and streaming with mud. But the mouth was clear, and after that first wailing cry the lips moved slowly, like a crab's, spitting out mud and roots.

Half an hour passed before the lump moved again. As it moved, the reeds away to either side of it bulged upwards and heaved, and the black, watery mud streamed through them. The mouth opened and a long booming groan came out of it, as the head hoisted clear. Another groan became a wailing roar. A seagull blowing across the marsh like a paper scrap veered wildly upwards as the streaming shape reared in front of it, like a sudden wall of cliff, pouring cataracts of black mud and clotted, rooty lumps of weeds where grass snakes squirmed and water voles flailed their forepaws, blinking their eyes and squealing as they fell.

The black shape was the size of two or three elephants. It looked like a hippopotamus-headed, gigantic dinosaur, dragging itself on all fours up out of a prehistoric tar pit. But now, still like a dinosaur, it sat upright. And all at once it looked human – immense but human. Great hands clawed at the head, flinging away squatches of muddy reeds. Then, amid the gurglings and suckings, and with a groaning wail, the thing stood erect. A truly colossal, man-shaped statue of black mud, raking itself and groaning, towered over the lonely marsh.

From *The Iron Woman* by Ted Hughes

Thinking back

Copy these sentences and put them in the correct order.
- As she lay on the ground Lucy heard a weird sound.
- When the bridge shook, Lucy thought it was an earthquake.
- Then, with a groaning wail, the thing stood erect.
- First the head came out of the mud.
- Lucy tried to run away but she tripped over.
- Next it sat upright like a gigantic dinosaur.

 Thinking about it

1 What made Lucy think it might be an earthquake?
2 What made Lucy jump up and begin to 'run blindly'?
3 What creatures did the 'thing' disturb as it came up from the muddy marsh?
4 At what point did it become clear that the 'thing' in the marsh was human-looking?

 Thinking it through

1 Did you enjoy this passage? Why?
2 Would you call this story a 'nail-biter'? Why?
3 Write some of the descriptive words, phrases or sentences the author uses.
4 a) Why do you think the Iron Woman was in the marsh?
   b) How had she got there?
   c) Do you think she had been in the marsh for long?
   d) Do you think she is friendly or fierce? Why?

UNIT 9 The Kangaroo's Coff

The eminent Professor Hoff
Kept, as a pet, a Kangaroo
Who, one March day, started a coff
That very soon turned into floo.

Before the flu carried him off
To hospital (still with his coff),
A messenger came panting through
The door, and saw the Kangarough.

'O Kangaroo,' the fellow said,
'I'm glad you're not already daid,
For I have here (pray do not scoff)
Some stuff for your infernal coff.

If you will take these powdered fleas,
And just a tiny lemon squeas
Mixed with a little plain tapwater
They'll cure you. Or at least they ater.'

Prof Hoff then fixed the medicine,
Putting the fleas and lemon ine
A glass of water, which he brought
The Kangaroo as he'd been tought.

The Kangaroo drank down the draught,
Shivered and scowled – then oddly laught
And vaulted out of the armchair
Before the Prof's astonished stair –

Out of the window, in the air
Up to the highest treetop whair
He sat upon the topmost bough
And chortled down, 'Look at me nough!'

From *The Kangaroo's Coff* by **Anthony Thwaite**

Thinking back

Copy and complete these sentences.
1 Professor Hoff kept a _____ as a _____ .
2 One day in _____ the kangaroo began to _____ .
3 The kangaroo had to be taken to _____ .
4 A messenger told the kangaroo to add a squeeze of _____ to some powdered _____ and mix it with some _____ .
5 When the kangaroo drank the medicine he _____ and
_____ .
6 Then he _____ and _____ out of the armchair.
7 The kangaroo jumped onto the top of a _____ .

Thinking about it

1 Where do you think the poem is most likely to be set – in Britain or Australia? Give your reasons.
2 What is unusual about keeping a kangaroo as a pet?
3 Could a kangaroo really be taken to a hospital?
4 What was unusual about the 'medicine'?
5 What effect did the medicine have on the kangaroo?
6 Did this surprise the Professor? How can you tell?
7 How do you think they will get the kangaroo down from the tree?

Thinking it through

1 Write some things you liked or disliked about the poem.
2 Why do you think the poet misspelt some words?
3 What can you learn about English spelling from this poem?
4 What do the following words mean? Use a dictionary to help you: a) eminent b) infernal c) scowled d) vaulted

UNIT 10 The First Man to Swim the Channel

Think ahead

What do you think might be the problems facing a cross-Channel swimmer?

Introduction

The shortest point across the Channel from England to France is about 34 km. It seems no distance at all on a cross-Channel ferry but to swim it is a different matter! There are many problems to be faced, such as energy-sapping coldness, monotony, attacks from jellyfish and getting tangled up in masses of drifting seaweed. The weather can change quickly too. The Channel is also the world's busiest seaway. On top of this there are strong tidal waters to be overcome too. In spite of all these difficulties, many have attempted it. This is the story of Captain Matthew Webb – the first man ever to swim the Channel.

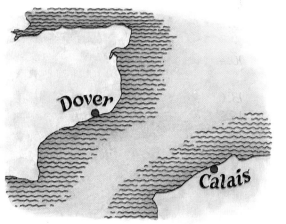

Key events in the life of Matthew Webb

1848   Matthew Webb was born in Dudley, Shropshire, near the River Severn, (where he learned to swim).

1856   By the time he was eight, Matthew was already a good swimmer. In this year he rescued his younger brother from drowning.

1860   Matthew loved the sea. He joined a naval training ship and soon became interested in long distance swimming.

1873   Matthew was awarded a medal for trying to rescue a sailor who had fallen overboard.

1875   After a successful career in the merchant navy, where he rose to the rank of Captain, he left in order to begin training to swim the Channel – his burning ambition.

Extracts from a report on Webb's cross-Channel attempt

Tuesday 24 August 1875

12.55 pm Captain Webb dived off Admiralty Pier, Dover, and started his epic swim with a slow steady breast stroke of twenty to the minute.

4.00 pm Had covered 8 km, battling against the NE tidal stream. The porpoises were very playful.

8.03 pm Sea calm. Swimming very strongly. Trouble with drifting seaweed.

9.20 pm Badly stung on shoulder by yellow star fish.

11.45 pm *Maid of Kent* passed close by. All 300 passengers cheered Captain Webb.

00.45 am Only 12 km from French coast but SW tidal stream making progress very slow.

03.00 am Change in weather. Strong breeze blown up.

05.25 am Voice of Webb faltering. Given hot beef tea to drink.

06.25 am Tidal stream too strong. Drifting. No progress

07.25 am Within sight of land. Still no progress.

09.40 am Stroke weakening, shorter and quicker – 26 to minute.

10.30 am Almost there.

10.40 am Matthew Webb reached Calais. Because of tidal currents, instead of 34 km, Webb had swum 61 km.

Thinking back

1 List five problems faced by cross-Channel swimmers.
2 Where was Matthew Webb born?
3 Where did he learn to swim?
4 What happened when he was eight?
5 When did Matthew Webb become interested in long-distance swimming?
6 Why was Matthew awarded a medal in 1873?
7 What rank was he when he left the Merchant Navy?
8 On what date did Captain Webb swim the Channel?

 Thinking about it

1 Where do you think Matthew's youngest brother might have been swimming when he nearly drowned?
2 Why do you think Matthew joined the navy?
3 List some of the problems encountered by Webb on his cross-Channel swim.
4 a) What do you think the *Maid of Kent* was?
  b) Why would Webb have been encouraged when it passed him?
5 How can you explain the fact that Webb actually swam 61 km instead of 34 km?
6 How many hours was Webb in the sea?

 Thinking it through

1 Why do you think Matthew Webb developed such a strong ambition to swim the Channel?
2 Name two occasions during the swim when Webb would have been a) encouraged b) discouraged. Explain why.
3 What do you think the following mean: a) battling against the NE tidal stream b) voice of Webb faltering?
4 What do you notice about the way the report on Webb's swim is written?
5 Why do people risk their lives attempting things never before attempted?

UNIT 11 The Business Letter

OFFICE FOR NATIONAL DATA COLLECTION

The Secretary
Fidgets Ltd
14 Rust Avenue
Luton Bedfordshire
LU3 9RX

Government Buildings
Bristol Road
Newport
Gwent NP22 2XG

Ref: 22617/455891/1998
Tel. Contact:
Mary Gray 01633 996541
25 October 1998

Dear Contributor

Your company has been selected to contribute to an annual business survey being carried out by this Office.

The survey is being undertaken to collect sales information on manufactured products within the European Community. The information is an important element of the Government's National Accounts on which major economic policies are based.

We appreciate the burden that the completion of the enclosed form may place upon small businesses such as yourself. In order to minimise the burden on businesses with fewer than 10 employees, if you complete the forms, no further forms for any business survey run by this office will be sent to you for the next three years.

A member of our staff will be contacting you in the next few weeks to confirm the exact nature of your business, to explain what information is required and to deal with any questions you may have.

Under the Statistics of Trade Act 1947 you are obliged to respond to our request for data by January.

Thank you in advance for your help.

Yours faithfully

J D French.

John D French (Director)

29

Thinking back

1 Who wrote the letter?
2 What is his job?
3 Where is his office?
4 What is the name of the company the letter is addressed to?
5 Where is the company situated?

Thinking about it

1 Why do you think the letter is addressed to 'The Secretary' and not to a specific person?
2 What have you learnt about Fidgets Ltd?
3 What is the main purpose of the letter?
4 Why is the information that is required important?
5 What promise does the writer make to the Fidgets company?
6 Why do you think they make this promise?
7 What does it say is likely to happen in the next few weeks?

Thinking it through

1 Look at the information at the top of the letter. List some of the clues given here that tell you this is a formal business letter.
2 Why does the writer sign off the letter in the way he does?
3 The writer speaks in a very formal and business-like way in the letter. Write an example of a fairly formal sentence contained in the letter.
4 Write the last paragraph in a more friendly way as if you were talking to someone you know well. Do it like this: I'm afraid that you've got to give me the information I ask for. The Statistics and Trade Act of 1947 says …

UNIT 12 Twelfth Night

The sea-shore. A storm-battered boat lies on the beach and, beside it, some half dozen survivors from the shipwreck: among them is a young woman, Viola.

VIOLA What country, friends, is this?

CAPTAIN This is Illyria, lady.

VIOLA And what should I do in Illyria? My brother, he is in Elysium. *(She gazes sadly out to sea.)* Perchance he is not drowned: what think you, sailors?

CAPTAIN It is perchance that you yourself were saved.

VIOLA O my poor brother! and so perchance may he be!

CAPTAIN True, madam, and to comfort you with chance, assure yourself – After our ship did split, I saw your brother bind himself to a strong mast that lived upon the sea. I saw him hold acquaintance with the waves so long as I could see.

VIOLA For saying so, there's gold! Knowest thou this country?

CAPTAIN Ay, madam.

VIOLA Who governs here?

CAPTAIN Orsino.

VIOLA Orsino! I have heard my father name him. I'll serve this duke. Thou shalt present me as a servant to him …

The captain nods, and Viola clasps him gratefully by the hand. So Viola, with the captain's help, becomes Cesario, a page, and attired as a man, serves the duke in his palace.

COURTIER If the duke continues these favours towards you, Cesario, you are like to be much advanced; he hath known you but three days and already you are no stranger.

The duke enters. Viola gazes at him, and it is evident that her feelings towards him are somewhat stronger than those of a page for his master.

DUKE Cesario, thou knowest no less but all: I have unclasped to thee the book even of my secret soul. *(He goes to the window and gazes towards the mansion of Olivia.)* Therefore, good youth, address thy gait unto her, be not denied access, stand at her doors, and tell them, there thy fixed foot shall grow till thou have audience.

VIOLA Say I do speak with her, my Lord, what then?

DUKE O then unfold the passion of my love.

VIOLA I'll do my best to woo your lady. *(She takes her departure, glancing back at the lovesick duke.)* Yet … who'er I woo, I myself would be his wife!

From *Twelfth Night* by William Shakespeare, adapted by Leon Garfield

➡️ *Thinking back*

Think of a good ending for each sentence.
1 Viola is a survivor from _____ .
2 The survivors are in _____ .
3 Viola's brother _____ .
4 Orsino is a _____ .
5 Viola becomes one of Orsino's _____ .
6 Viola dresses as a _____ .
7 Viola falls in love with the duke but he is in love with

_____ .

8 Olivia lives in a nearby _____ .

Thinking about it

1 Were there more than six people on the boat before it was wrecked? How do you know?
2 How do you think the boat was wrecked? What evidence is there in the text?
3 Why does Viola gaze sadly out to sea?
4 What do you think the captain means in his lines which begin 'True, madam ...'?
5 Why do you think Viola changes her name and appearance to become a page to Orsino?
6 Which lines spoken by the courtier, tell you that Cesario (really Viola) has already become a favourite of the duke?
7 Which line tells you that Viola has fallen in love with the duke?
8 Why does the duke send Cesario to see Olivia?

Thinking it through

1 What clues are there that this play was written many centuries ago?
2 What did you find strange about the language? How hard did you find it to understand?
3 Write the words or expressions below in modern English as we would say them, for example,
Knowest thou this country = Do you know this country?
a) what think you, sailors?   b) he hath known you but three days   c) I have unclasped to thee the book even of my secret soul   d) Address thy gait unto her   e) be not denied access
4 Why are some words written in italics?
5 Which famous playwright (author) wrote the original version of *Twelfth Night*?
6 Find out some more information about this famous playwright.

UNIT 13 Amanda

Think ahead

In this poem Amanda is getting told off by her Mum. What sort of things do you always get told off about at home?

Don't bite your nails, Amanda!
Don't hunch your shoulders, Amanda!
Stop that slouching and sit up straight,
Amanda!

(There is a languid, emerald sea,
where the sole inhabitant is me -
a mermaid, drifting blissfully.)

Did you finish your homework, Amanda?
Did you tidy your room, Amanda?
I thought I told you to clean your shoes,
Amanda!

(I am an orphan, roaming the street.
I pattern soft dust with my hushed, bare feet.
The silence is golden, the freedom is sweet.)

Don't eat that chocolate, Amanda!
Remember your acne, Amanda!
Will you please look at me when I am
    speaking to you,
Amanda!

(I am Rapunzel, I have not a care;
life in a tower is tranquil and rare;
I'll certainly never let down my bright hair!)

Stop that sulking at once, Amanda!
You're always so moody, Amanda!
Anyone would think I nagged you,

Amanda!

From *Amanda* by Robin Klein

Thinking back

Complete these sentences spoken to Amanda by her Mum.
1 Don't bite _____ .
2 Don't eat _____ .
3 Stop that _____ .
4 Don't hunch _____ .
5 Remember _____ .
6 Will you please _____ .
7 I thought I told you _____ .
8 Did you finish _____ ?
9 Anyone would think _____ .
10 Did you tidy _____ ?

 Thinking about it

1 Do you think Amanda always does as she is told?
  Give reasons for your answer.
2 You can learn quite a bit about Amanda from this poem.
  For example, Amanda bites her nails. Write down five facts
  you can discover about her.
3 How does Amanda usually respond to her Mum's nagging?
4 Do you think Amanda's Mum is always nagging her? Say why.
5 Write five things you can discover about Amanda's Mum
  from the poem.

 Thinking it through

1 How can you tell who is saying what in the poem?
2 Do you think Amanda does her fair share of the jobs around
  the home?
3 Do you think children should help around the home? Why?
4 Would it be true to say that Mum's concerns are for the real
  world but Amanda is a bit of a day-dreamer? Give your
  reasons.

UNIT 14 In the Stable: A Christmas Haiku

Think ahead

Look at the title, the picture and the headings at the beginning of each verse. What is the poem going to be about, do you think?

Donkey
My long ears can hear
Angels singing, but my song
Would wake the baby.

Ox
I stand patiently.
It is busy here tonight.
Who is this baby?

Sheep
On bleak hills my wool
Keeps me warm. Is your baby
Snug enough in straw?

Camel
I have brought treasure
But kneel now to the maker
Of sun, moon and stars.

Dog
I will not bark but
Lie, head on paws, eyes watching
All these visitors.

Mouse
In this place I feel
Safe. This baby will not scream
If he sees quiet me.

Cat
I wash my feet. For
This baby all should be clean.
My purr will soothe him.

Spider
My fine web sparkles:
Indoor star in the roof's night
Over the baby.

Owl
My round eyes look down.
No starlit hunting this night:
Peace to the little ones!

Dove
I decorate this
Manger with an olive branch.
It promises peace.

From *Writing Poems* by Michael Harrison

36

Thinking back

1 How many animals are mentioned in the poem?
2 Where are all the animals?
3 What can the donkey hear?
4 What is the cat doing?
5 How does the mouse feel?
6 Is the camel kneeling or standing?
7 What is the dove decorating the manger with?
8 Where is the spider?

 Thinking about it

1 Why are all the animals keeping very quiet?
2 How will the cat soothe the baby?
3 What has the owl given up to be in the stable?
4 What does the poem tell you about the hills around the stable?
5 Why do you think the camel says that it has brought treasure?
6 In what way is the spider's web like a star?
7 What visitors do you think the dog is watching?
8 Explain what a 'stable' and a 'manger' are.

 Thinking it through

1 Did you like the poem? Write your views about it and give your reasons.
2 This poem does not rhyme. Does this matter? Explain your answer.
3 How many verses are there?
4 In what way is this poem like a conversation or a little play?
5 This is a particular type of poem called a *haiku*. Each verse contains exactly seventeen syllables in total. Each line always contains the same number of syllables. Count the syllables in each line and explain what you have discovered.

UNIT 15 Christmas Dinner

Think ahead

*This passage is about a Victorian family's special Christmas Dinner.
What is the best meal you have ever had? What was so special about it?*

Mrs Cratchit made the gravy (ready beforehand in a little
saucepan) hissing hot; Master Peter mashed the potatoes with
incredible vigour; Miss Belinda sweetened up the apple sauce;
Martha dusted the hot plates; Bob took Tiny Tim beside him in a
corner at the table; the two young Cratchits set chairs for
everybody, not forgetting themselves, and mounting guard upon
their posts, crammed spoons in their mouths, lest they should
shriek for goose before their turn came to be helped.

At last the dishes were set on the table, and grace was said. It was
succeeded by a breathless pause, as Mrs Cratchit, looking slowly all
along the carving knife, prepared to plunge it into the breast; but
when she did, and when the long expected gush of stuffing issued
forth, one murmur of delight arose all round the board, and even
Tiny Tim, beat on the table with the handle of his knife, and feebly
cried Hurrah!

There never was such a goose. Bob said he didn't believe there
ever was such a goose cooked. Its tenderness and flavour, size and
cheapness, were the themes of universal admiration. Eked out by
the apple sauce and mashed potatoes, it was a sufficient dinner for
the whole family; indeed, as Mrs Cratchit said with great delight

(surveying one small atom of bone left upon the dish), they hadn't ate it all at last! Yet everyone had had enough, and the youngest Cratchits in particular, were steeped in sage-and-onion to the eyebrows!

But now, the plates being changed by Miss Belinda, Mrs Cratchit left the room alone – too nervous to bear witness – to take the pudding up, and bring it in.

Suppose it should not be done enough? Suppose it should break in turning out? Suppose somebody should have got over the wall at the back yard, and stolen it, while they were merry with the goose; a supposition at which the two young Cratchits became livid! All sorts of horrors were supposed.

Hallo! A great deal of steam! The pudding was out of the copper. A smell like washing day! That was the cloth. A smell like an eating house, and a pastry cook's next door to each other, with a laundress's next door to that! There was the pudding. In half a minute Mrs Cratchit entered: flushed but smiling proudly: with the pudding, like a speckled cannonball, so hard and firm, blazing in half of a half-quartern of ignited brandy, and bedight with Christmas holly stuck on top.

Oh, a wonderful pudding! Bob Cratchit said, and calmly too, that he regarded it as the greatest success achieved by Mrs Cratchit since their marriage. Mrs Cratchit said that now a weight was off her mind, she would confess that she had had her doubts about the quantity of flour. Everybody had something to say about it, but nobody said or thought it was at all a small pudding for a large family. It would have been flat heresy to say so. Any Cratchit would have blushed to hint at such a thing.

At last the dinner was all done, the cloth was cleared, the hearth swept, and the fire made up. The compound in the jug being tasted and considered perfect, apples and oranges were put upon the table, and a shovel-full of chestnuts on the fire. Then all the Cratchit family drew round the hearth, in what Bob Cratchit called a circle, meaning half a one. The chestnuts on the fire sputtered and crackled noisily.

Then Bob proposed:

'A merry Christmas to us all, my dears. God bless us!'

At which all the family re-echoed.

'God bless us every one!' said Tiny Tim the last of all.

From *A Christmas Carol* by Charles Dickens

Thinking back

Write and say if each statement is true (T), false (F) or you can't tell (CT).
1 Mrs Cratchit made the gravy in a saucepan.
2 Master Peter mashed the parsnips.
3 The kitchen was big.
4 They had turkey for dinner.
5 Everybody had enough to eat.

Thinking about it

1 List all the people who were at the Christmas dinner.
2 Why was there a 'murmur of delight' as Mrs Cratchit cut the goose?
3 What expression tells you that the youngest Cratchits were full up?
4 What compliment did Bob Cratchit pay his wife?
5 In your own words, describe the pudding.

Thinking it through

1 How can you tell the passage was written last century?
2 Write down a few of the words that you did not understand and say what you think each might mean.
3 Describe what you imagine Mrs Cratchit to be like.
4 What sort of picture do you think the author was trying to create in this passage for the reader?
5 From which book did this passage come? Who wrote it? Find out some more about this author.

UNIT 16 The Fuss over the Fordham Factory

Think ahead

Read the introduction and the newspaper article.
What sort of arguments do you think the people of Fordham
will put in favour of the factory and against it?

Fordham Common is a large area of open land just on the outskirts of
the town. There are no other big recreational areas like it nearby.

THE FORDHAM TIMES

Factory to be built on Fordham Common

On Thursday the local planning committee gave planning permission for a biscuit factory to be built on Fordham Common. Mr Norman, the Chairman of the Committee said, 'This will bring new business and jobs to our town. It is a chance we cannot afford to miss. The people of Fordham will soon get used to the idea. The Common will make an ideal site for the factory.'

It's not fair, we'll have nowhere to play football.

Many of the local residents are opposed to the idea. They decide to write letters to their local Member of Parliament and to the local council and the *Fordham Times*. They protest outside the Town Hall. (One protester even chained herself to the Town Hall door!) They stick posters up everywhere giving their point of view.

But, like most arguments, there is always another side to the story. Not everyone in Fordham is against the factory!

Melvyn Smart is a local builder looking for more work. He would like to help build a large new factory.

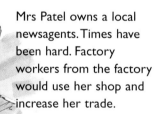

Mrs Patel owns a local newsagents. Times have been hard. Factory workers from the factory would use her shop and increase her trade.

Tracey Saunders is a teenager. She hasn't been able to find a job. She feels the factory would bring extra jobs to Fordham.

PC Sharma, the local policewoman, feels the factory will bring more life into the area.

Mr Timms, the Head Teacher of the local school, is sure that the factory will bring more children to his school.

Thinking back

1 What is Fordham Common and where is it located?
2 What sort of things is the Common used for?
3 What are the plans for the future of the Common?
4 Where did many people read about the plans?
5 Give three reasons against the factory.
6 Give three reasons for building the factory.

 Thinking about it

1 Why do you think the Planning Committee gave permission to build the factory?
2 What is the point of protesting?
3 Think of some other reasons against building the factory.
4 Which person do you think has the best reason for wanting the factory built? Why?
5 Think of some other reasons why people might want a factory built on the Common.

 Thinking it through

1 Write what you think the top three arguments against the factory are, in order.
2 Write what you think the top three arguments for building the factory are, in order.
3 Which side of the argument do you agree with most? Why?
4 There are often good reasons for both points of view. Sometimes a compromise is reached which tries to satisfy both sides. Suggest a way of solving this problem, so that both sides are satisfied.

UNIT 17 There's a Dragon

Think ahead

Read the first line of the poem.
What do you think it is going to be about?

There's a dragon in a motor car,
a dragon, so it's said,
a dragon in a motor car
that fills the air with lead.

There's a dragon in a chimney stack,
a dragon, it's no joke,
a dragon in a chimney stack
that fills the sky with smoke.

There's a dragon in the ocean waves,
just watch its limbs uncoil,
a dragon in the ocean waves
that drowns the birds in oil.

There's a dragon by the river bank
who has an evil wish,
all day it drivels toxic saliva
that kills off all the fish.

There's a dragon underneath the ground
whose power will not pass,
it sweats out noxious chemicals
that poison crops and grass.

There's a dragon in the power station,
all year it quietly breathes,
there's a dragon in the power station
that could fill whole towns with wreaths.

There's a dragon in the heart of man,
invisible as a rule,
there's a dragon in the heart of man,
the most dangerous dragon of all.

From *There's a Dragon* by **Charles Thomson**

Thinking back

Complete each sentence with an appropriate ending.
1 The dragon in the motor car fills the air with _____ .
2 The dragon in the chimney stack fills the sky with _____ .
3 The dragon in the ocean waves drowns the birds in _____ .
4 The dragon by the river bank kills off all the _____ .
5 The dragon underneath the ground poisons _____ and

_____ .
6 The dragon in the power station could fill whole towns with

_____ .

Thinking about it

1 What is the 'dragon' being referred to in the motor car?
2 What harm can smoke cause?
3 How did the 'dragon' in verse 3 get into the ocean?
4 Where do you think the 'toxic saliva' on the river bank has come from?
5 What do you think 'noxious' and 'wreath' mean?
6 What do you think verse 7 means?

Thinking it through

1 Are the 'dragons' in the poem good or bad dragons? Why? What is this poem really about?
2 What do you think of the way the poet uses the word 'dragons'? Is it effective? Why?
3 What other creature or creatures could the poet have used as metaphors instead of dragons?

UNIT 18 Trash or Treasure?

Think ahead

If you are untidy, then you will be able to relate to Joe Gardener.
His desk was like a rubbish tip!

I peered in the dark abyss that was Joe Gardener's desk. 'How can you ever find one special sheet of paper in that tip?'

Flushing, he tried to defend himself. 'I'm looking for my dictionary as well.'

I dipped my finger in and gingerly stirred a few mucky papers about. 'No sign of any books in here.'

'Maybe it's sunk to the bottom.'

'Why don't you clear it out, for heaven's sake? Then you'd be able to find things.'

He said unhappily, 'I do try. it's just – ' His voice trailed off. It didn't matter, though. I didn't really need telling. I'd seen him take a million years to (try to) write three words. If someone like Joe tried clearing his desk, he'd have a beard down to his feet before the job was done.

I pushed my blank 'How-to' book cover aside. 'All right,' I sighed. 'Let's get on with it.'

'But we're supposed to be ...'

I didn't stop to listen. I just punted up to the front to fetch the waste paper bin. Miss Tate's beady eye fell on me the moment I stretched under her desk.

'Howard?'

'Just borrowing the bin,' I explained.

'But, Howard, that bin's for everyone.'

I think what I hate most about being in school is being treated like a half-wit.

'Yes, I do understand,' I said. 'But right at this moment, Joe and I need it most because he can't get down to work until we've cleared out his desk and found his dictionary.'

A strange light flickered in her eyes. 'Cleared out Joe Gardener's desk?'

I think I got the look right. I think my expression clearly said, 'Yes, lady. You get the pay cheque. I do all the work.'

No more trouble from her, then. I carried my trophy back and planted it on the floor beside Joe's desk. Then I pointed to my chair. 'You sit here.' He shifted over. (Putty in my hands!) 'Right,' I said, lifting out the first sheet of chicken-scratchings. 'Trash or treasure?'

'Trash,' he admitted.

I lifted another. 'Trash or treasure?'

'Trash.'

This is my mother's trick. She uses it on me three times a year, before my grandmother's visits. 'What about these?'

'Trash. Trash. Trash. Trash. Trash.'

It took a while. I had to keep putting my foot down to stamp the rubbish down, and make more room. But gradually we worked our way down all the tides of rubbish in his desk. And once or twice we had a nice surprise.

'Treasure! I lost that pound weeks ago!' or 'My dental appointment card! Mum's been nagging me for that!'

And, suddenly, a triumph!

'Hey. That's my special sheet of paper!'

'Take a break.'

I strolled across to Flora. 'Borrow your sticky tape?'

Miss Tate had spotted me. 'Howard,' she trilled. 'We don't go wandering in this class without putting up our hands first, to ask permission.'

What is it with teachers and this stupid 'we' business? Miss Tate had been rolling round the room all morning, and never once put up her hand.

'Gosh, sorry,' I warbled, and scuttled back with Flora's tape in hand. I used a lot. (No point in messing about.) I stuck that special piece of paper on the desk so well it won't go walkabout again. And I took a look at it.

once	knew	called	guess
ready	caught	night	garden
school	hospital	break	doing

That sort of thing. And maybe I was in a mood because I hadn't had time to get started on my own work. 'Oh, right,' I muttered. 'All the really hard words.'

Joe lifted his face. 'That's right,' he said gratefully. 'All the words where it's easy to make mistakes.'

So I admit it. Though I didn't smirk, I was still feeling pretty superior as we ploughed through the silt at the bottom of his desk. 'Trash or treasure?'

'Trash.'

'Into the bin. And this?'

He reached for it in relief. 'My dictionary!'

'Just try to keep it near the top in future.' (Miss Tate could take lessons from me.) 'Is that the lot?'

He took the last thing I was holding up. 'Trash.'

He dropped it in the bin, and was about to put his foot on it when I reached down and snatched it. 'What is this?'

'It's just a photograph.'

'I know it's a photograph, Bean brain,' I told him sharply. 'But what is it?'

'It's just a model I made last year.'

'Just a model?' I inspected it. Then I inspected him.

'Excuse me,' I said. 'But may I ask you a very personal question? If you can make a three metre model of the Eiffel Tower from macaroni, why can't you keep your desk tidy?'

'I don't know.'

I was still staring at him when the bell rang. I hadn't got any work done. But I'd achieved something. I'd shifted a major health hazard in the next desk. I'd got to know the worst writer in the world. And I'd worked out he wasn't daft.

Not bad for my first morning, you'll admit.

From *How to Write Really Badly* by Anne Fine

Thinking back

1 What is the name of the person who was writing the story?
2 Who does he sit next to at school?
3 What is the name of their teacher?
4 What did Howard help Joe to do?
5 What system did Howard use to help Joe decide whether to keep something or throw it away?
6 List some of the 'treasures' the two boys found.
7 Apart from keeping his desk tidy, what else does Joe have difficulty with at school?
8 Name something that Joe is good at.

 Thinking about it

1 How can you tell Howard was new to the school?
2 What did Howard mean when he said:
   a) 'I peered into the dark abyss that was Joe Gardner's desk.'
   b) 'If someone like Joe tried clearing his desk, he'd have a beard down to his feet before the job was done.'
3 Howard doesn't have a very good opinion of Miss Tate. How can you tell?
4 What can you learn from the passage about
   a) Howard?   b) Joe?   c) Miss Tate?

 Thinking it through

1 Did you like Howard? Give your reasons.
2 How did you feel about Joe? Say why.
3 How did Howard help Joe feel better about himself?
4 Did you like the author's style? Give your reasons.
5 Did you think there was anything unusual about the way the story was written?
6 How can you tell the story is American? What evidence is there?

UNIT 19 Sleep

Think ahead

What time do you go to bed? How much sleep do you get most days?

1 Why do we sleep?

We all need to sleep to allow our bodies to rest and to recover from the rigours of the day. Our bodily systems must have time to rest and relax. If we don't sleep properly we can become tired, clumsy and sluggish the following day, and find it difficult to concentrate.

2 _____

If we have a very late night or our regular sleeping patterns are disturbed we can feel quite strange. When people travel in aeroplanes and across the world's time zones they may suffer from 'jet lag' because the 'time clocks' inside them have become temporarily mixed up. It takes a while to adjust.

3 _____

Sleeping patterns do tend to change with age. We seem to need different amounts of sleep at different times in our lives. New-born babies sleep most of the day. As we get older, people seem to need less sleep. When people reach their 60s many find it harder to sleep for eight hours a night - but they also find it difficult to stay awake for a whole day! That's why they may have a nap during the day at some point.

4 _____

Most healthy adults would say that a good eight hours' sleep is important if they are to function effectively. Different creatures sleep for different amounts of time each day. Horses sleep for just three hours each day. A rabbit may sleep for about the same amount of time as the average human. A cat snoozes for twelve or more hours a day whilst hamsters clock up to fourteen or so hours every day. Squirrels sleep even longer (up to seventeen hours each day) – but one of the champion sleepers must be bats. They sleep an amazing twenty hours every day!

5 _____

Each time we fall asleep we enter a cycle of different stages that repeat themselves throughout the night. Scientists have identified four different stages to our sleep cycle. The first stage is the transition between being awake and being properly asleep – when we 'drop off'. Stage two is known as normal sleep. Stage three is another 'in between' transition period which moves us into the next stage. Stage four is when we fall into our deepest sleep. After we fall asleep we reach Stage four quite quickly. It is this kind of deep sleep that we need to refresh ourselves.

6 _____

In 1952 it was discovered that at some points during the night our eyes dart about beneath our closed eyelids. It is as if we are following imaginary moving objects with our eyes. This is known as 'REM' or Rapid Eye Movement. This happens when we are dreaming. Scientists believe that dreaming is an important part of sleeping, too. They suggest that babies spend about half of their sleeping time dreaming. Scientists also think that most mammals, birds and reptiles also dream whilst asleep.

Thinking back

1 Why do we need to sleep?
2 What happens if we do not get enough sleep?
3 What is 'jet lag'?
4 What happens to the amount of sleep we need as we get older?
5 How much sleep do most healthy humans need?
6 Which animal sleeps   a) least?   b) most?
7 How many different stages are there in our sleep cycle?
8 Why is the kind of sleep we get at Stage four so important?
9 What does REM mean?
10 When does REM happen?

 Thinking about it

1 The first paragraph has been given a title. Think of a suitable title for each of the other paragraphs in the passage.
2 Why do you think you find it difficult to concentrate if you don't have enough sleep?
3 Why do you think new-born babies sleep so much?
4 Place the following in order, according to how much they sleep each day:
   humans, hamsters, horses, cats, bats, rabbits, squirrels.
5 What do you think the following mean:
   a) rigours b) sluggish c) temporary d) transition e) rapid
6 Think of some synonyms for the word 'sleep'.

 Thinking it through

1 Stories are usually written in one continuous text.
   a) This information text is broken down into headed sections.
   b) Why do you think this is? How helpful is it?
2 How useful are the pictures in helping you understand better? Why?
3 List some of the problems scientists may face in trying to understand what happens when we are asleep.

UNIT 20 Cluny's Army

Think ahead

Read the introduction and look at the picture. What clues are there that tell you this story is not going to be about a human army?

The mice in Redwall Abbey live in peace until they are attacked by the terrible rat Cluny the Scourge and his army. Matthias, a young mouse, soon finds his dream of becoming a warrior is a grim reality.

Cluny knew the value of fear as a weapon. And Cluny was a fearsome figure.

His long ragged black cloak was made of batwings, fastened at the throat with a mole skull. The immense war helmet he wore had the plumes of a blackbird and the horns of a stag beetle adorning it. From beneath the slanted visor his one eye glared viciously at the Abbey before him.

Matthias' voice rang out loud and clear from the high parapet, 'Halt! Who goes there?'

Redtooth swaggered forward and took up the challenge in his Chief's name, as he called back up at the walls, 'Look well, all creatures. This is the mighty horde of Cluny the Scourge. My name is Redtooth. I speak for Cluny, our leader.'

Constance's reply was hard and unafraid, 'Then speak your peace and begone, rats.'

Silence hung upon the air while Redtooth and Cluny held a whispered conference. Redtooth returned to the walls.

'Cluny the Scourge says he will not deal with badgers, he will only speak with the leaders of the mice. Let us in, so that my Chief may sit and talk with your Chief.'

Redtooth dodged back as his request was greeted by howls of derision and some loose pieces of masonry from the ramparts. These plump little mice were not as peaceful as they first looked.

The rats looked to Cluny, but he was eyeing the Abbot who had joined Constance and Matthias. They appeared to be consulting quietly. Cluny watched tensely; there seemed to be some disagreement between the old mouse and his two advisers. They conferred awhile; then Matthias came forward to the parapet. He pointed at Cluny and Redtooth with his staff.

'You there, and you also. My Abbot will talk with you both. The rest must remain outside.'

A rumble from the horde was silenced by a crack from Cluny's tail. He lifted his visor.

'We agree, mouse. Let us in.'

'But what about hostages for safe conduct,' hissed Redtooth.

Cluny spat contemptuously. 'Don't talk wet. D'you imagine a load of mice in funny robes could take me captive?'

Redtooth gnawed anxiously on his split claw. 'Maybe not, Chief, but have you cast a weather eye over that badger?'

Cluny answered quietly out of the side of his mouth. 'Don't worry. I've been watching her. A real big country bumpkin. No, these are mice of honour, they'd sooner die than break their word to anyone. You leave this to me.'

As Cluny and Redtooth made for the gatehouse door, Constance shouted, 'Put down your weapons, rats. Throw off your armour and show us you come in peace.'

Redtooth spluttered angrily. 'Hell's teeth! Who does that one think she's ordering around?'

Cluny shot him a warning glance. 'Quiet. Do as she says.'

Both rats took off their armour and placed it in a pile on the road. Matthias cried down to Cluny, 'If you really are Cluny the

Scourge, then we know of your tail. It is a weapon. Therefore you will knot it tightly around your waist so it cannot be used.'

Cluny laughed mirthlessly. He squinted at Matthias and cracked his tail dramatically.

'Young mouse,' he called. 'You do right to ask for this thing, for truly you are looking at Cluny the Scourge.'

Having said this he took his tail

in his claws, and pulled the poison war spike from its tip. Tossing it on the armour pile, Cluny hitched his tail in a knot around his middle.

'Now will you let us in, mice? You can see we are unarmed.'

Ponderously the heavy gate inched open. The two rats passed through a bristling forest of staves. The gate slammed shut behind them.

Cluny mentally estimated the walls to be of immense thickness and he and Redtooth, ducking their heads, emerged from the tunnel-like arch into the abbey grounds, where Constance and Matthias were waiting in the sunlight. The defenders followed the two rats closely, menacing them with staves.

Matthias rapped out a curt command, 'Leave us, mice. Go back to your duties on the wall.'

Unhappy at leaving the Abbot unguarded, the mice hesitated to obey the order to withdraw. Cluny addressed Matthias scornfully, 'Here, mouse, watch me shift 'em.'

Suddenly he whirled upon the apprehensive creatures. The single eye rolled madly in its socket as Cluny bared his claws and fangs, snarling, 'Ha harr! I've got a powerful hunger for mice! You'd best get aloft on those walls. Ha harr!'

Cluny leapt in the air. The mice scattered in panic.

From *Redwall* by Brian Jaques

 Thinking back

1 What kind of animal was Cluny?
2 What was Cluny's nickname?
3 What was Cluny wearing?
4 Who was Redtooth?
5 How did the mice react when Redtooth asked to be let in?
6 Who did Matthias say could enter the Abbey?
7 Which character was worried about entering the Abbey – Redtooth or Cluny?
8 What did Constance demand that Redtooth and Cluny did to their armour?
9 Why was Matthias concerned about Cluny's tail?
10 How were the mice in the Abbey armed?

Thinking about it

These sentences outline the main events in the story but they are mixed up. Write them in the correct order.

- The Abbey gates were opened to allow the two rats to enter.
- Constance demanded that Cluny and Redtooth took off their armour.
- Cluny and his army approached Redwall Abbey.
- Cluny leapt in the air and made the mice scatter in panic.
- Matthias said that Cluny and Redtooth could enter the Abbey without their army.
- The mice were unhappy to leave the Abbot unguarded.
- Matthias insisted that Cluny tie his tail around his waist.
- Constance and Matthias met Cluny and Redtooth when they came in the Abbey.

 Thinking it through

1 The author paints a vivid picture of Cluny. Write your impression of him. Describe his appearance and write some sentences about the sort of person he was.
2 It is possible to learn some things about the other characters in the story as well. Look for the clues and write two sentences about each of the following, saying what you have learnt about them:
   a) Redtooth   b) Matthias   c) Constance   d) the Abbot
3 Answer the following questions about the setting of the story:
   a) What do you know about the Abbey?   b) Who was in it? Why?   c) Why do you think Cluny wanted to attack it?
4 Use a dictionary to help you write the meaning of these words:
   a) swaggered   b) squinted   c) visor   d) contemptuously
   e) ramparts   f) hostage   g) horde   h) conference

UNIT 21 Robinson Crusoe's Diary

Think ahead

Why do people keep diaries? Do you think Robinson Crusoe's diary is a modern diary or one written some time ago? How can you tell?

Daniel Defoe wrote a book about a character called Robinson Crusoe who was shipwrecked on an island in the West Indies. He wrote it in the form of a diary. The story was so convincing and realistic that many people thought it had really happened! Here are a few entries that he kept in his diary about his time on the island.

1659

<u>September 30</u>   I, poor miserable Robinson Crusoe, being shipwrecked during a dreadful Storm, came on Shore in this dismal unfortunate Island, which I called the Island of Despair, all the rest of the Ship's company being drowned and myself almost dead.

I had neither Food, House, Clothes, Weapon or Place to fly to. In Despair of any Relief, I saw nothing but Death before me, either that I should be devoured by wild Beasts, murdered by inhabitants or starved to death for Want of Food.

At the Approach of Night, I slept in a Tree for fear of wild Creatures.

<u>October 1</u>   In the morning I saw to my great Surprise my Ship had floated with the high Tide and was driven aground much nearer the Island. I hoped, if the wind abated, I might get on board to fetch food and Necessities.

<u>October 24</u>   I have spent this three Weeks getting all I could out of the Ship and bringing it on Shore on a Raft. I now have Guns, Gunpowder, Pistol, Sword, Axe, Saw, Nails, Ropes, Blankets, Clothes, Sails, a Hammock, Biscuits, Flour, Rum, Wine, a Bible, Pen and Ink, and three or four compasses.

   And I must not forget the two Cats and the Captain's Dog Japp. He jumped out of the Ship and swam on shore with me.

<u>October 25</u>   I cut a Post. On its Side, I cut every day a notch and every seventh day I made a long line and at the end of every month I made a cross. Thus I keep my Kalendar and yearly reckoning of time.

<u>October 26</u>   I walked about almost all Day to find a place to fix my House. I was greatly concerned to secure myself from Attack in the Night either from wild Beasts or Men. Towards Night I fixed on a Place under a Rock and marked myself out a Semi-Circle for my Camp which I planned to strengthen with a Wall or Fortification.

<u>November 5</u>   This Day I went with my Gun and my Dog, and killed a wild Cat, her Skin pretty soft but her flesh good for nothing. Coming back by the Sea Shore, I saw many Sorts of Sea Fowls which I did not know but was surprised and almost frightened by two or three Seals which, while I was watching, got into the Sea and escaped me.

<u>November 23</u>   I have been working all these days to make my Cave into a Storehouse, Kitchen, Dining-room and Cellar. I sleep in the Tent outside. When it rains I cover the Tent with long Poles leaning against the rock. I cover the Poles with Plants and Leaves like a thatched Cottage.

1660

April 17   I was terribly frightened by the most surprising
Thing indeed. All on a sudden I found the Earth come
crumbling down from the Roof of my Cave and two of the
posts I had set up cracked in a frightful manner. I was
heartily scared thinking my Cave was falling in and I should
be buried in it. I climbed out over my Wall.

I was no sooner stepped down upon the firm Ground than
I saw it was a terrible Earthquake. The Ground I stood on
shook three Times at about eight Minutes Distance with
such Shocks as would have overturned the strongest
Building. A great Piece of Rock fell down with such terrible
Noise as I never heard in all my Life. The very Sea was put
into violent Motion by it and I believe the Shocks were
stronger under the Water than on the Island.

I was so amazed that I was like one dead or stupefied.
And the Motion of the Earth made my Stomach sick like
one that was tossed at Sea.

Then it rained most violently so that I had to cut a hole
in the Wall of my Fortification like a Sink to let the Water
out, which would else have drowned my Cave.

From *Robinson Crusoe* by Daniel Defoe

 Thinking back

1 a) Who wrote the book? b) Who was the main character in
   the book? c) What was special about the way in which the
   book was presented? d) Why did many people believe it was
   a real story?
2 What happened to Robinson Crusoe at the beginning of
   the book?
3 What years are covered in this extract from the diary?
4 What pet animals swam ashore with Robinson Crusoe?
5 How did he keep a record of the time as it passed?
6 Make a list of the things Robinson Crusoe managed to bring
   ashore from the wreck of the ship.
7 What did Robinson Crusoe do when it rained?

Thinking about it

1 How can you tell Robinson Crusoe is feeling very sorry for himself on September 30?
2 What were his main concerns on his first day and night on the island?
3 Why would Robinson Crusoe have been surprised and pleased to see that the ship had not sunk completely?
4 What did he have to read on the island?
5 Why do you think Robinson Crusoe felt it was important to keep track of time?
6 Why did he plan to strengthen his camp with a wall or fortification?
7 Describe the sequence of events that took place on 17 April 1660.

 Thinking it through

1 Is Robinson Crusoe just interested in recording facts in his diary? Give reasons for your answer.
2 He doesn't record something on every day. Why do you think this could be?
3 What do you notice about the way Robinson Crusoe uses capital letters?
4 Apart from the dates, how can you tell the diary was written several centuries ago? Provide evidence for your answer.
5 Find the following words in the diary and say what you think they mean:
a) dismal   b) devoured   c) inhabitants   d) abated
e) hammock   f) notch   g) stupefied

UNIT 22 The Mysterious Postcard

'Well, I'm blowed,' Father said, picking up the postcard off the floor. 'What do you make of this, then?'

'Of what, dear?' said Mother, wiping her hands on her apron, and coming to look over his shoulder.

'Can't hardly make it out,' said Father, peering at it closely. 'It's funny writing, don't you think? Anyway, seems we're all invited to some sort of family reunion. Never heard of such a thing, have you?'

'What's it say?' I asked, looking at the picture on the back of the postcard. It was the Tower of London with a Beefeater standing outside looking very serious.

'It says: "To the Family Throckmorton" – that means you too, Jimmy.' Little Jim waved his arms up and down like a tin drummer boy and then rubbed his soggy rusk in his ear. 'It says: "You are all invited to attend a grand reunion of our family to be held at the Tower Hotel, London, on the fourteenth of July at noon. Have your name writ upon you so we may know one another." '

'Very mysterious,' said Mother. 'I wonder who sent it. Can't spell, whoever it is. Should be "written" not "writ". And it's not signed at all. Just look at that writing, Bess. Worse than yours.' And she turned the card round to show me. The handwriting was all squeezed up and tall. I could hardly read a word of it.

'Rum business if you ask me,' said Father. 'Could be a hoax for all we know.'

'Nonsense,' Mother said. 'People have family reunions all the time. I think it's a lovely idea. I'd love to go – but the fourteenth – I think something's happening on the fourteenth.' And she went over to look at the calendar by the telephone. 'Oh dear, I thought so. We can't go, not on the fourteenth. You've got to see the accountant in the afternoon, dear. Little Jim's got his diphtheria jab in the morning at the doctor's. And you were coming with us, Gran, for your check-up, remember? What a pity.' Gran was about to protest. 'It would be too much for you anyway, Gran. You know what the doctor said about overdoing it. And Will's still away at camp with the school. Where did they say they were having it?'

'The Tower Hotel, it says here,' said father. 'Up in London. Somewhere near the Tower of London, I suppose.'

'That's where they cut off all those heads,' said my brother Will, doing up his trousers as he came in the door. 'I've seen the very place where they cut off their heads. I've seen the axe. Sharp as a razor it was. Mind you, one of them Beefeaters said it sometimes needed three or four swipes if your neck was a bit thick.'

'Will!' said Mother. 'That's quite enough. Now sit down and eat your breakfast!' She turned to me. 'But you can go, Bessy. If we could find someone to take you, you could go.' I shook my head. I didn't like parties at all and there'd be lots of strange people. 'Bound to be lots of other children there,' Mother went on. 'You'd like to meet your cousins, wouldn't you?' I wonder if Aunt Ellie got an invitation. She'd take you. I know she would.'

The telephone rang, and Mother was right beside it. It was Aunt Ellie, and yes, she'd had an invitation. No, hers wasn't signed either, and yes, she'd take along anyone who wanted to go. Everyone told me I should go. 'Nothing ventured, nothing gained,' said Gran. 'Be interesting,' said Mother. So I went.

As it turned out the party wasn't a bit interesting, not to start with, anyway.

From *My Friend Walter* by Michael Morpurgo

Thinking back

Choose the correct word to complete each sentence.
1 There was a picture of (Buckingham Palace/Tower of London) on the postcard.
2 The postcard invited the family to a (reunion/pantomime).
3 The (writing/picture) on the postcard looked all tall and cramped.
4 It wasn't possible for anyone in the family to go except (Gran/Bess).
5 Then (Aunt Bess/Aunt Ellie) telephoned and said she was going.

Thinking about it

1 How can you tell father is surprised when he picked the card up?
2 How can you tell Little Jimmy got excited when father spoke to him?
3 Why did Mother think the card was 'very mysterious'?
4 Describe what you think Gran is like. (Look for clues in the passage!)
5 Why did Mother tell Will to be quiet?

Thinking it through

1 Which of the family members is telling the story? How do you know?
2 Who do you think sent the postcard? Are there any clues in the passage?
3 The invitation is to a family reunion. Do you think there is more to it than that? Why?
4 How can you tell the card is from someone back in history?
5 Look at the last sentences in the passage. Why do you think the author ends like this?
6 What sort of things would Bess be thinking about as she went to the reunion?